FIGHTING

by Xavier Coy

ORiGiN™
Theatrical

FOR ALL ENQUIRIES CONTACT: ORiGiN™ Theatrical
PO BOX Q1235, QVB Post Office, Sydney, NSW, 1230, Australia
Phone: (61 2) 8514 5201
enquiries@originmusic.com.au   www.origintheatrical.com.au
Part of the ORiGiN™ Music Group
An Australian Independent Music Company

IMPORTANT NOTICE

should not be considered to be necessarily endorsing or otherwise attempting to promote an affiliation with any of the owners of the brand names or trademarks or public figures. Such references are solely for use in a dramatic context.

LANGUAGE NOTE

Licensees are welcome to make small alterations to the language that is used is this play so as to make it suitable for a younger cast and/or audience.

MUSIC USE NOTE

Licensees are solely responsible for obtaining formal written permission from copyright owners to use copyrighted music in the performance of this play and are strongly cautioned to do so. If no such permission is obtained by the licensee, then the licensee must use only original music that the licensee owns and controls. Licensees are solely responsible and liable for all music clearances and shall indemnify the copyright owners of the play(s) and their licensing agent, ORiGiN™ Theatrical, against any costs, expenses, losses and liabilities arising from the use of music by licensees. Please contact the appropriate music licensing authority in your territory for the rights to any incidental music. In Australia and New Zealand, contact APRA AMCOS apraamcos.com.au.

If you are in any doubt about any of the above then contact ORiGiN™ Theatrical.

For complete listing of plays and musicals available to perform and all licence enquiries, contact ORiGiN™ Theatrical.

www.origintheatrical.com.au
+ 61 2 8514 5201

iii

AND HERE ARE THE RULES
IN PLAIN ENGLISH FOR YOU...

<u>DO NOT</u> perform this play without getting permission from ORiGiN™ Theatrical first. In 99% of cases you'll need to pay us money to be allowed to stage a performance. This money goes to the author(s) of the show who shed blood, sweat and tears creating this play. Please don't rob them of their livelihood.
Go online www.origintheatrical.com.au or call +61 2 8514 5201

<u>DO NOT</u> make a copy of this book by photocopying, scanning, taking a photo, retyping (on a computer or a typewriter), or using a pencil, pen or chalkboard. If you want to purchase more copies contact ORiGiN™ Theatrical.
Go online www.origintheatrical.com.au or call +61 2 8514 5201

<u>DO NOT</u> make any changes to the text without first getting permission from ORiGiN™ Theatrical in writing. Sometimes you'll be allowed to make changes and sometimes you won't. Please always check with us first.
Go online www.origintheatrical.com.au or call +61 2 8514 5201

<u>DO NOT</u> record your performances or rehearsals in any way without first getting permission from ORiGiN™ Theatrical. We know everyone wants to try and record everything on their phones these days. We get it. But please don't encourage them or give them permission. Sometimes there are important contractual reasons as to why we can't give you permission to record it. And sometimes there aren't any reasons and we can say YES. Please just check with us first.
Go online www.origintheatrical.com.au or call +61 2 8514 5201

<u>DO</u> contact ORiGiN™ Theatrical if you have any questions about anything. At all. And we mean anything. One of us that works here (not me) has a peculiar interest in recording the unusual bird calls of the adult hoatzin (a species of tropical bird found in wet forest and mangrove of the Amazon and the Orinoco delta in South America) so we should be able to answer any questions you have about the Hoatzin. Plus we know some things about some other things too.

Thank you for taking the time to read this.

AUTHOR'S NOTE

One the first day of COVID lockdown in March of 2020 I was diagnosed with Bipolar Disorder. It led me down a path of introspection and self-discovery. It also elucidated a lot about the world we're in and how we view this disease. When I was first diagnosed I was confronted with many different responses. Some people accepted me and wanted to help and know more. Others went into denial, others were upset and didn't want to talk about it and then others had no idea what it was.

Since my diagnosis I have come to learn what Bipolar really looks like and how it is represented on stage and screen. It borders on confused to wrong to offensive. So much of it is generalized "crazy". Seeing all this led me to write 'Fighting' as a way of showing an authentic experience of the disease from my perspective. Everyone's Bipolar is different but it's important to experience the disease from the life of someone who actually has it.

I've always believed that in order to reach people that comedy is a great tool. 'Fighting' blends dry comedy with the true darkness of what it's like to live with a disease that can take you down at any point. I set the play over the course of a day in order to show just how persistent you have to be to keep on top of your brain. It's work. It challenges you.

COVER ARTWORK BY MICHAEL ARVITHIS
@michaelarvithisartist

'I'm so happy because today
I found my friends
They're in my head
I'm so ugly, but that's okay, 'cause so are you'

'Lithium' by Nirvana

Three actors split this text. One person plays the protagonist the whole way through and the other two actors interchange between the voices in his head and characters in the scenes.

Black.
Not black – blue. Dark blue.
Must be the middle of the night.
Early morning.
We could argue all day.
All morning.
See – the sun – it's coming – it's black – so dramatic.
I'm a little – what's the word I'm looking for?
Foggy.
Give me a better one.
Discombobulated.
No, no, not so much effort. Let it roll off the tongue. Cool. But also expressive.
There's one thing we can agree upon – I'm awake.
Whether that's good or bad is a judgement call.
If we're dealing in facts – plain and simple – you're awake.
That pulling –

Tension.
In your solar plexus.
Tell me what it looks like.
I haven't even got out of bed –
Tell me.

Sandstone. A big lump of sandstone. It takes up three quarters of my torso but it's heavy – coarse to the touch. It's by the edge of the water. A piece juts out across the edge, any closer and it'd surely tip. But it doesn't. It stays there. On the edge.

Beat.

2

I need coffee.
Is that such a good idea?
I have coffee everyday.
It's not helping with your sleeping.
I'm hardly sleeping anyway.
What's that stuff they gave you?
Quetiapine.
Should knock out a horse.
Then why can't they do the job on me?
You're large though. Larger than average. Not a dig.
It's good to be honest with yourself.
Ya fat cunt.
So, we're off to a flyer.
Fresh start.
Blinding pace.
Remember when waking up used to be exciting?
No one likes a glib prick.
What's glib? It's nostalgia. Good times.
Like the time you fell into the bushes on that first date and
impaled yourself on the tree branch. The ambulance came. You
punctured your liver remember?
Yeah…
You have to laugh don't you?
She didn't call back did she?
Did we settle on coffee?
Yes.
No.
I need it.
Offset with a five milligram valium.
Benzo's are cool.
Not helpful.
Like, addictive, but you got worse issues.
Cool. Just a fiver.
Uh-huh no benzo's in the morning.
They're a band aid.

Band aids are okay.
At least try to start the day without them.
But –
You're admitting defeat before the fight.
All I do is fight.
Ohhhh darling.
Just one valium.
No.
Fine. Just coffee. No valium.
Are you sure you're capable of having coffee today?
Hey, here's an idea, shut the fuck up for a second.
Wow what are you fifteen? Is that your retort?
Positive strides.
Routine is key.
I'm taking a fiver for the road.
If you must.

Step One. Medicate.

Puffer.
Hilarious.
Lamotrigine. Mood stabilizer for the morning.
Great for the depressive side of things but the mania –
Lithium. Save that for night time. Second mood stabilizer.
Meant to be the gold standard in –
Are they working?
You've got exercises.
LOL.
They'll bring you on an even keel.
Even-ish.
And the ADHD meds?
Not today.
Running the gauntlet.
Loves a challenge.
Get on with it.

Step Two. Shower.

Hit the perfect balance, the water's hot enough to bring a pink
hue to the surface of my skin, enough for my body to register
that something's happening but not enough to cause pain.
I edge the hot a little more – maybe I can take it. I can.
Go on.
A little more.
The heat and the pressure, it hits the back of my neck and rolls
down my shoulders, like the water's embracing me.
Been a while since you've had an embrace isn't it?
Got a date tonight, dickhead.
Third one and no embrace – not even a kiss on the cheek.
There was a wave from a metre away on the second date.
Progress.
The pressure, the heat, I'm awake. Furiously tired but awake.
Shit takes it out of you.
Just a bit more.
Fuck. Fuck. Fuck. Too much.
Back down and now I'm freezing.
The bathroom window, even though only ajar, feels like it's
blowing a gale – freezing my scolding body. I'm pink and
shivering.
Like a naked mole rat.
Pretty.

Step Three. Clothes.

Remember you chafe in those undies.
Wear the comfy undies.
Not those ones. What are they Ed Hardy? Are you a bikie on
holiday in Thailand?
They're not Ed Hardy.
How long have you had them – there's a hole in the gooch bit.
Alright, how about these?

5

Right.

Are we that out of options?
Kind of.

I haven't done washing in a -
No one'll be seeing them so I guess –
Go for it.
They're good.

Great. You're going with the black jeans aren't you?
I was thinking of maybe mixing it up today.

Beat.

Yeah I was thinking the black jeans.
And the same shirt –
Yeah and that shirt.
Whatever makes you comfortable.
I think I look good in this. Hey I was thinking – my friend told
me I should look into doing some things to pamper myself. She
told me that women on death row put on make up to make
themselves feel good. Like they've got a routine.
You want to put make up on?
No just do something nice for myself.
What does that look like?
Well I'll need to think.
Okay, think.
Give me a second.
You brought it up.
Yeah I know –
But you didn't have any answers?
I was canvassing the idea.
You could start by making your bed.
That's not pampering.

Dusting. There's a lot of dust in here.
When was the last time you vacuumed?

Step Three. Breakfast.

Step, four dickhead. You've done step three.
Muesli, no brainer, let's move on.
Well just hold on a second.
Please.
No, no, it's worth discussing. Carbs.
You need carbs.
Big boy needs carbs? With his metabolism?
I'm having muesli and milk. That's it.
Milk doesn't agree with everyone.
It does with me I've been having muesli and milk everyday for
the last five years.
You had that friend –
I'm fine.
Went to the doctor and what did he say?
I don't remember.
She'd been drinking cappuccinos but had a stomach that was so
averse to dairy that she had a metre of poo log jammed inside
her.
Again, I'm fine with milk.
As far you know.

Step Five. Leave The House.

Phone. Keys. Wallet. Headphones. Puffer. Phone. Keys. Wallet.
Valium. Keys.

What have I forgotten?
Brush my teeth.

Better.

Phone. Keys. Wallet. Headphones. Fuck where'd I put my – back pocket. Phone. Keys. Wallet. Headphones. Puffer. Valium.

Okay. Here we go.

Coffee.

Hey, the usual?
Long black with a drop of –
Cold milk.
Thanks.
Big night?
Sorry?
Your eyes are red – puffy – you look hungover.
Oh. I've been crying.

Beat.

Yeah.
Like, I'm fine. I have bipolar. So sometimes – I'm fine.
That's the one – bipolar – hey that's um –
I probably shouldn't have told you that.
No it's – I mean it's –
Like, you're not my friend.
Okay.
I mean you are my friend. I guess. But you're mostly my barista.
Your barista.
My barista friend who makes my coffee of a morning.

You've paid?
Yeah.
There's your coffee.
Thanks. See you tomorrow.

I can never go back there again.
Poor barista.
I didn't mean to –
She's a really talented artist. Look her up on Instagram.
What's her name?

You're a piece of shit.

Wow she is incredible.
Vectors.
Heaps of vectors.
Invisible lines that draw your eye –
I know what vectors are.
Testy.

Phone rings.

Hi Mum.
Same time, same thing. On my way to work.
No I didn't ask for a raise.
Well because I'm the worst salesman in the shop. Yeah but they don't care if I'm a nice person. In fact it probably works against me.
Okay I'll ask today.

Shit no I didn't. How old is he now? Yeah I know he's my cousin I just – he's fucking nine? When did that happen?

How are you?

Probably for the best. I have to go – I'm just about to walk into
work – I'll ask.
I love you too. Yeah I'll talk to you later. I will.
Promise.
Bye, Mum.

You should call her more often.

You should do a lot of things you don't do.
Cook more.
Eat more vegetables.
Read.
I read.
Not enough.
Learn another language.
Learn the salsa.
I can't salsa.
You could try.
Yeah I could. But I'm not going to.
We know.
Hard enough getting out of bed in the morning.
Sad sack of shit.

Welcome to my brain.

Is that a Charles Manson quote?
Or Ted Bundy?
Fine line isn't it?
No it isn't.
What's that?
It isn't.
Between sane and insane.
There's a very clear line.
I'm on the right side of the line.

Onya, Ted.

I have to go into work.

Work.

You're disappearing again.
Look up – take it in.
Gets harder each day.

The sky disappearing.
Fading into the obscurity of being another nothing. Another
nobody.
Caked on smiles.
General Pants employees pretending the thumping music is fun.
Boost workers trying not to thrust their hand into a working
blender.
Muffin Break employees…Looking genuinely happy.
Must be the smell of the muffins.

You've walked past it all and you're met with -

Fluorescent lights.
The smell of plastic.
Generic corporate rectangle.
You're wasting your life.
And behind the desk is Helga. A rotund woman in her sixties
who thought a sensible career change meant opening up a
Vodafone franchise with her gaunt seventy five year old
boyfriend Clifford.

You look tired. We've got to get you sleeping properly don't we?
Um. Yeah. That's the plan. Is Clifford off again?

No he's running late. We had sex this morning and he did his back again. He'll be in he just needed to find his Meloxicam.

Oh yeah – Helga and Clifford have sex a lot.

I hope he's okay.
We're fine if we do doggy style or the missionary position. It's the adventurous maneuvers that get us into trouble. We tried to have sex in the shower again.
Yeah, okay, that's gross.
I've got bad knees you see –
You've told me.
So bending – it's not really an option. So he was doing the lion's share of the work this time around.
Did we get in any new screen protectors?
That's not to say I don't contribute.
Please. Fuck.
I do.

You look tense.
I feel tense.
Still not having sex?
Just talking about it a lot.
Every couple has their dry spells.
I'm not in a relationship.
Oh, bugger it, she dumped you didn't she?
A year ago, Helga.
I thought you were trying to work it out?
I was trying to work it out.
Well...The grass is always greener...
Grass is pretty brown here.
Good one! You're funny.
I'm a riot.

You'll find someone.

Cliff arrives.

Morning!
Morning, Cliff.
You look terrible.
I'm hearing that.
What's wrong with you?
Nothing's wrong.

Got no poker face, chief.

I've always loved your inability to deflect.
Such grace and subtlety.

Now, now, what's wrong?

Fucken nothing cunt. You're wrong.

You can tell us. We're your employers but we're also your
friends.
I don't really feel comfortable –
We're here for you.

Well I guess…I've been in a bit of rut with my um – a trench – a
gulley. I thought I was good but then, you know, there's the
other side of good. There's happiness staring you in the face and
instead of taking it and spending time with it, you wrap your

13

arms around it so hard and and and you take every bit of oxygen from it – you want it to stay with you so badly that you just end up…killing it. Then what you're left with is this…lifeless…lump.

You know I might have a cup of tea. Would anyone else like one?
I need a cigarette.

Is smoking that bad for you?
Yes.
But –
Yes.
But –
Don't smoke.
I need a hobby.
Smoking isn't a hobby.
Why does it still look cool when people smoke?
It doesn't.
James Dean.
Seventy years ago.
Don't smoke.
Fine.

My god how is it only ten A.M.?

Sometimes when I look at Helga I get so overwhelmed I just want to hug her. I don't know why.
Like…In a platonic way?
Yeah she's lovely – I'm not saying – hang on what?
She's a sex goddess and you're -
Shut up.

Hot Helga.

There's something - It's not – she's happy. Like, she's cool with this. This job. This life. Her gangly, wrinkly lover. And for some reason that makes me…She smiles and – I don't get it. How do you just exist in this place?
How do you sell phones for a living and smile?
How do you sit under these lights – like you're some experiment – like you've been put here and everyone else around is part of the trick –
That's the Truman Show.
You can't dupe us.
Playing it off as if it was his idea.
Pretty sure once a movie's made, released to the public, become a massive international success and been a cult classic for over twenty years you can't claim original concept.
Wonderful.

She's so happy. And so's he.

What have we for morning tea, dear Helga?
Your favourite. Cabanossi and cheese.
Yum, bum, yummitty-yum-yum!
Shit, man, I've never been that excited about anything in my life as that old man is about cured meat.
This is the best thing I've ever eaten.
What have you got?
Banana.

Small one.
That's not going to fill you up.

Yeah, no, I don't even really like bananas.
Silly boy.

They're meant to help with serotonin.
Have you been running?
What?
We have a friend who tells us about her depleted serotonin after
going on runs. She runs half marathons. Fascinating woman.
Something about the salt.
That's magnesium.
We should have her around for dinner soon, Helga.
I'll call her this afternoon.
You should come too. Talk about your depleted serotonin levels.
Haha!
Sounds great.

Do you want some cabanossi?

Yes. Thank you.

Rank.

Shop's empty as per usual.
Doesn't bother me necessarily. Doesn't seem to bother Helga or
Clifford at all.
They're holding hands…
That's…
They're holding hands…

And even though that should warm my heart...All I can think
about is them fucking.

So we're all in agreement – there's issues there.
When have I denied that?
Just checking.
So gangly.
Stop.
I would if I could.
I should see if she's taking fish oil.
Why?
For her joints.
No, why? Why do you want to start this –

Do you take fish oil?
Pardon?
Fish oil. For your joints. Your bad knees.
Oh.

Yes. I do.
Cool.
Did you tell him about my injury?
No she/didn't.
/Yes.
Helga!
What?
It's embarrassing.
There's nothing embarrassing about our active sexual life.
No, my injury. It makes me sound like an old man.
You're not young.
Sorry I brought it up.
Stay out of this.
Yep.

I'm not much older than you.
Well, eight years.
Exactly.
I mean…That's significant enough.
Do I look like an old man to you?
Ahhhhhhhhhh –
Leave him alone.
Do I?
No?
Why did you say it like that?
I'm um – I feel I should say I regret the decision to bring up the fish oil.
We're past that. I'm an old sack of shit to you am I?
Clifford…
No –
Just because I have a pensioner's card doesn't mean I'm less of a person. In fact I get cheap bus fares so I may in fact be more important than the average Joe.
I'm not saying –
You could learn a thing or two from someone like me.
Definitely.
Don't patronize me.
I think you're a great – there's so much – I wish I could find um – Clifford, you're a…you're a beaut.

We can put this whole thing to bed now can't we?
I think so.
It's just good to know I'm respected.
Absolutely.
By both of us.
Especially me.
I think I'm more…Impressive to you.
You're most certainly impressive.
So are you.
Really?

I think so.
Good to know we impress each other.
Indeed.
What is it that impresses you?
Clifford...Stop...
Of course...

I need to go to the bathroom...
As do I...
Oh. Shall we walk there together?
Okay.

Good for them I guess.

Doesn't it depress you?
It's kind of hot.
Everything can change in an instant.
Oh yeah that's likely.
I want to be happy.
Walt Disney sort of happy? Off with the fairies.
Level.
Walt Disney was an anti-Semite. Do you want to be an anti-Semite?
Was he?
Hated Jews. Nazi man. Went to the meetings.
Shit a brick. I love Dumbo.
You don't have enough Jewish friends by the way.
Right.
Well...What does that say about you?
I dunno - how do I fix that? Go to a fucking synagogue and hand out my business card?
Don't be ridiculous.

You don't have a business card.
I could.
Oh yeah – 'Phone salesman' – that's good.
Selling your soul.
Make a pretty penny.
Just a penny.
Charge.
Go forth.
Relentless pressure.
Feel that? Ouch.
Scratching.

No. No. We're not doing this.

Sorry.

What are you sorry for?

It's just easier if I say it.
Yeah but you don't have any reason to apologize.
Now, sure, but historically I've probably done things I need to apologize for.
How does that have anything to do with now?
It has *everything* to do with now. It's why we're in this predicament.
I like that we're referring to it as a predicament. Kind of cute.

Quick thought. We should really look at a skincare routine.
With you on that.
Okay. Tomorrow.
Yeah, yeah, yeah.
Never a better time to start than the present.
You've got like…Cavernous pores.
Hectic.

Tomorrow.
Danger. Past and future. You're drifting.
Something's happening.
Look at your hand.
Shut up.
Little dance move.
Twitch.
Ah.
Twitch.
I can feel it.
Twitch.
You're cracking.
I'm not.
Think of something funny.
Or nice.
Pleasant.
Funny.
You're twitching.
Something funny.
Or nice.
Twitch.

My head.
Coming from the base of the neck.
Can we turn the lights off?
It's not a migraine.
No – the brightness is –
Stress. Relax maaaaaan.

He does this. The headaches. Always has. They thought he had a
tumor as a boy.
These headaches.
They couldn't figure it out.
Kept coming back and back and no one could figure it out.
MRI's come up clean.

Stress. Anxiety. Chill out, kid.

Hey, chill out.
Breathe.

What do we think about meditation?
Hearing good things.
So that means…
He's not gonna do it.

Think of something nice.
Treat it like an observational exercise. You can't ignore the darkness.
Acknowledge it.
Just don't engage.
Remember what it's like to have fun?
Don't be cruel.
Creature comforts.
Fun!

Wow. Nothing?
I'm thinking.
Fuck man.
Seriously?
Air hockey.

What?
You haven't played air hockey in like –
I enjoy it.
Okay. Cool. Air hockey.
Should we pop down to Timezone? Take on some eight year kid, ruin their week?
Two people crying playing air hockey, that's an image.

Hang on!

Timezone's gone out of business hasn't it?
Has it?
That's Blockbuster.
Oh what are we going to watch when we get home?

We could try getting into French New Wave cinema again?
HA!
Watching the first twenty minutes of something doesn't mean
you've seen it.
But you get the gist.
Better to know a little about a lot!
It's cool to know shit. Makes you interesting. Interesting people
reference things.
To make up for the fact they don't have anything to say for
themselves.

Introductions:

*I am more than you, I hope you understand that. I'm my own
person. I have a fully-fledged, wholly formed view of the
world…Though it may be misanthropic, it is mine and mine
alone. You might have your hands on the steering wheel but I
can turn it any point.*
Don't believe me?
*You're happy. Out for drinks. A couple too many. Shit, you're
even dancing. Badly but it's something.*
*You leave. You're walking down the street. You pass a man –
he's standing by himself. He looks angry.*
The better part says keep walking, no need to engage.
'Nice shirt.'
What did you think was going to happen?
*You keep walking but before you know it you're on the ground
and he's on top of you.*

The back of your head's bleeding, he clipped you with a good one.
He's dragged off you.
Bouncers take pity.
Only got yourself to blame.
If not for the kindness of others…
Lucky, right?
Yeah.
Instead you think…If only he'd really connected with that punch then maybe…

That's me. Kiss, kiss.

You've said your piece.
I've just started.
He's got work to do.
See the problem with your brain is –
- Let me count the ways –
I thought you were on my side?
I'm malleable.
The problem is that at some point in the process you are faced with a choice –
Chemicals.
You either continue down the path of destruction or you mend yourself.
It's not that simple.
Medicine.
The way I see it, you live for the destruction, you pine for agony, the only thing more soothing than getting love from others is hating yourself.
I'm working through some – I'm trying to change – I want to think differently.

Can't I just bury you?
Won't work.
I'll find a way back.

Cliff Returns

Sorry for leaving you on your lonesome, young man. You look worried. Were we inundated with new clientele?
No.
Oh well. Build it and they will come.

Helga and I just made love.
Good.
That's why we left. We said we were going to the bathroom but the truth of the situation is that weren't going to urinate…We were going to bonk.

Bonk?
Screw.
Right.
And screw we did.
Cliff I really don't –
Have you ever had Cialis?
No.
I'd recommend it.
Erections aren't the problem.
Oh what you've got to look forward to.
Yeah.
It'll happen to you.
Yeah.
I was just like that. Perhaps even more unflinchingly obstinate –
It's not obstinacy –

But things change. Your body starts to belie you and assistance is
needed.
Cool.
Don't be dismissive, it'll happen.
It's more I don't really want to keep talking about you and
Helga...Where is Helga?
She went up to Fitness First to have a shower.

You want to see him in action don't you?
No. Fuck.
Do you think anyone's ever orgasm'd in your company?
Doubtful.
Yes. They have.
When?

Heaps of times.
Yeah...

It's more than sex.
Sorry?
With Helga and I. It's more than sex.

I thought I should clarify that. We have a very earnest and
important connection. Our love making is just an expression of
that. To think it's just physical would be wildly underestimating
to power of what we have.

Disgust.

In the pit of your stomach.
Bile, tracking up your throat.
But you keep it down.
A washing machine. The latch is starting to crack open.
Tumbling around and around -

Thought you had them pegged.
Protecting yourself.
Everyone's in the same boat as you.
All your hard work – the assumptions.
Blasted.
Love.

Easy isn't it?
To pretend you know what happens behind closed doors.
Act as if you know someone.
Rather than investigate.
What's that saying?
Never judge a book by it's –
Blurb.
Only gives you a snippet.
Snippets aren't enough for value judgements.
Don't be so hasty to judge.
But be hasty enough to protect yourself.
Remember when you used to have fun?
Fun, fun, fun, I'm trying to…When was that?
Um…

Why don't you learn how to be fun?
We're treading dangerously close to –
Dream.
Uh-uh. No.
Close your eyes for a second. No one will see.
Avoidance.
Breathe.

I'm still here.
I can only help you so much.

You look tense.
Okay.
Are you tense?
Yes.
Why?
I'm a tense person.

Yeah, I'm tense. I'm really tense. I'm so tense I -

Diazepam.
See the wonderful thing with valium is it'll stop the full blown
panic attack that was almost inevitable but it won't stop the brain
from coming back and pushing, pressure on the back of your
skull, rolls around to the front – you start seeing spots and
BANG.
But it'll stop the panic attack.
Twenty minutes before relief.
But until then you're on your own.

The Other Introduction:

You're not doing this alone. I'm here. And that thing over
there – well they're here too. But you and I, we battle together.
Trust me.
Here – you're six years old. You're at a fate, standing at the
spinning wheel to win a prize. For some reason all you wanted
was a leg of ham. I'm not saying you were a normal kid –

besides the point. You wanted that ham so badly. While your sister was spending her allotted cash on rides you were spending yours on the hope you'll get ham.
All that enthusiasm, all that hope, all that excitement at seeing the wheel spin around and around – all that joy...That's me.
And remember when you won the ham? You were the happiest little kid that's ever been.
You won a ham half your size.

Actually I really do think I have to set the record straight – not because I wasn't happy for you I just – I think it makes it even better actually. They gave you that ham out of pity. You spent all your money and the market value of the ham was actually less than what you spent so...People care. They care about you.
Do you remember that joy?
That's me.

And the anxiety, the agitation, the no sleep. Don't pretend we're on different sides.

Shit, Cliff, he's talking at me.
In case you haven't noticed, Cliff, despite working in communications, is remarkably poor with emotions.

Your eyes are a bit misty.
Yeah.
Are you about to cry?
Hopefully not.

If you do need to cry probably best to do it outside the shop.
Customers...
I might be okay if we stop talking about it.
Fine. Fine.

Do you see someone to help with your problems?
Yes.
A shrink?
A psychologist, yeah.
You know I haven't cried in years. Is that strange do you think?
Um –
I wouldn't imagine it's all that healthy? I suppose I've always
suppressed my emotions come to think of it. My father was a
sailor. We never spoke of our feelings. He saw things at sea…If
I'm honest with myself I think he preferred marine life to
humans. Do they call that Daddy problems?
Not clinically.
Do you do exercises in these shrink sessions?
Sometimes, yeah.

Maybe you could teach me some of them.
I wouldn't really feel comfortable –
Why not?
Well, Cliff, I'm not a psychologist.
No…But –
I'm not a psychologist.
You could still teach me.
I don't want to.
Jeez.
I wouldn't feel comfortable. I'm not a psychologist.
Yes, I'm aware, I thought of it more from a generosity of spirit
point of view.
Right.
But if it makes you so uncomfortable –
It does.
Well then…

Do you still need to cry?
No. I'm good.
I'm glad I could be here for you.

Do you ever think to yourself how the fuck did I get here? Where
did the last five years go? Am I kidding myself that the potential
I saw in myself is still there? I'm sure I had it once. I'm
positive…

Be happy with your lot.

People come in dribs and drabs.
Do you need a hand with anything?
No thanks.

A group of fourteen year old's are perusing the newest iPhone.
It's not even worth it.
How much is this?

I hate myself for even giving it breath –
On a plan or outright?
What am I doing? No one's ever signed up to a new phone plan
while simultaneously drinking a slushie.

What's the difference?
On a plan the phone comes with it –
Is that what I really sound like?
- But if you just want the phone you can pay for just the phone
and sign up to a plan or prepaid separately.
Cool.

So how much is it?
We've got some of the earlier models on sale for seven hundred and fifty dollars.

Cool.

How much data does it come with?
Depends on the plan.
And so, the new one's, like, really expensive?
Well it's more than seven hundred and fifty dollars so…

Cool.
Bye.

Bye.

Helga's return is, by this point, welcome. And with frazzled sex hair she looks a picture of happiness.
That's nice isn't it? Seeing a Boomer smile.
Boomer's a derogatory term now.
Isn't it factual?
No, but, you know, the tone has changed. The intent.
When did this happen?
I saw an article on the Huffington Post. People are really taking offence.
You wouldn't want to offend anyone would you?
Ageist.

Did we get any customers?
Not yet sweetheart.

Cliff…Professional.
Oh. I beg yours. Not yet, Helga…You sexy thing.
Cliff!
Was that naughty?
Yes!
Is that a problem?
…No.

Loneliness.
Belly button – an arrow shot through your core.
An expansive field – there's an oak tree in the middle of it –
towering. Solitary. Leaves falling, you see the base begins to
shrink; the tree begins to wither before –

Customer. Time to step up.
Helga and Cliff are lost in each other; adoringly staring so deep
into each other's eyes they're almost hypnotized.
It's a woman. She's in a suit. She looks impressive. Slightly
stern. Or maybe that's my perception – my bias – my lack of
confidence – my lack of –
She's getting closer.
Just relax.
Your hand.
I know. I know.
Deep breaths.
Done it a million times.
Fucked it up a million times too.
Not untrue.
Double negatives – why?
I'm not steering this ship.

She's getting closer –
Step by dreadful step.

The click of her kitten heels like the sound of beating drums.
You're desperate for an exit.
And now –
She's here.
There.
Right in front of you.
Waiting.

Are you going to speak?

Hi, hello.
Two greetings – someone's lucky day.
Hi there.
How can I help you?
She's already incredulous – she should've gone to Optus.
I need a new iPhone.
Jesus Christ people are predictable.
Sure thing. We've got the newer models out on the floor here
and I've got some of the older ones out back that are slightly
cheaper.
Remember Blackberry's?
I'll get a new one.

His voice breaks slowly like a pubescent boy.

Fantastic.

Someone has to acknowledge that.

Excuse me.
What for?

For the…
Did you sneeze?
It was a reflex.
What was?
Excusing myself.
What were you excusing yourself for?
My, um, when my voice – I had a testy pop.

A testy pop?
A break in my voice.
Right. I didn't hear it.
It was quite loud I thought.
Well…There you go.
You didn't hear it?
Didn't hear it.
Okay.

So I didn't really need to excuse myself?
I don't know why you want to keep talking about it.
She really scares you, hey?
Neither do I.
Then stop.
I will.
Great.

iPhone.
Sheep.
It's also worth mentioning that the new Samsung is –
I'm not interested in a Samsung. I want an iPhone.
In a lot of ways the Samsung is superior to the –
I want an iPhone.
Should've finished that business degree.
Well if you're sure.

I'm sure.
Idiot. You. Me. This is an idiotic conversation.
Can you shut up?
Excuse me?
Not you.
What?
Doesn't matter.
Well, I mean, you did just tell me to shut up so –
No I – I told myself to shut up.

Would you like to go to dinner? Joking. You'd never ask that.

Do you…hear voices?

Not really voices…More thoughts…
I might do some shopping and/I'll come back.
/You'll come back. Yeah. Sure.

The one that got away.
So close.

Despair.
Wrists. Like a wringing, joints feel like they're crumbling.
A silo – pieces of grain cascading, slipping down the sides.
Quicker and quicker. No point grasping – everything's
falling away –

Do we think it's time for lunch?
I brought the rest of that spag bowl, Helga.
Did we not agree to have that for dinner?
No, not to my knowledge.

Slightly selfish not to ask.
Would you like some?
How much is there?

That's all there is?
I had a midnight snack.
Good-o.
Are you upset with me?
Oh no I'm not upset, Cliff.
Good.
I'm not upset with your incredibly selfish and thoughtless
behaviour.
Helga…
I'm not upset, Cliff. Why would I be upset? It's not like spaghetti
bolognaise is my favourite meal and the unspoken rule of
cooking together is unless stated otherwise we go halves in
things – why would I be upset?
This seems to be a slightly extreme reaction to a bit of spag
bowl, Helga.
How dare you. How very dare you.

Did you bring lunch?
I always mean to but –
Come on. My shout.
Really?
If I have time to question it I might renege.
Coming.

Get a burger.
Sushi.
Pizza.
Salad.

Kebab.
On a Tuesday at lunchtime? Way too rogue.
Indian.
Vietnamese.

Do you know what you want?
I think I'm going to get a juice.

You'll regret that.

Just a juice?
I'm trying to watch my calorie intake.
…Okay.

Sitting here with Helga, amongst the chaos, the unknown, I
feel…Comforted. There's a tenderness. She looks at you and you
get the sense that she really cares. And I have to admit…That
look is very welcome.

She's gone with KFC and…I'm kind of jealous.

How's your juice?
Delicious. How's your zinger?
Just what I needed.

This isn't going to fill me up.

Do you want a chip?
Don't.
Yes please.
I got a large because I knew you'd still be hungry.

God she's good.
Still wish I didn't know as much about her sex life –
But – chips.
True.

Thanks, Helga.
You're very welcome.

Under normal circumstances silences in conversation make me
jittery. It feels like a failure on my part – we've run out of things
to say – the conversation has come to a staggering halt because
I'm not interesting enough to sustain a back and forth.
With Helga…It's kind of peaceful.

Can I tell you your problem?
Must you?
From a place of love.
Like that makes it better. No offence, get off the fence, off!
Sometimes I think you're a little –

I know. Of course I know. I spend all day in this fucking head.
You're not going to present me with any insight. Chaos and
cruelty. So pathetic.
The boy who couldn't even muster the energy to be angry – sits
in sadness.
I wish I was angry.
No you don't.
Yes. At least there's force in anger. There's momentum, there's
– misery is pithy and pointless.

I think you're a little hard on yourself.

Interesting.

We're all hard on ourselves.
Not to the point of...Put your hands on your chest.
Why?
Just do it.
We're in the middle of lunch.
It'll only take a second.
My hands are all dirty.
You only had a juice and a chip. Close your eyes.

Hands go on chest.

Now, breathe into your hands.
I don't know what you mean by that.
Picture your breath going down into your lungs and filling them
up. Can you picture it?
Not really.
Concentrate.

Yeah, I can picture it.
Now imagine – concentrate –
I am.
Imagine that breath is softening your body, your hands are
sinking into your chest and you're wrapping your hands around
your heart. Is this making you uncomfortable?
Yes.
Good. In your hands take your heart, gently, and hold it.
I feel sick.
Keep your eyes closed.

Helga, really –
Trust me.

Take your heart – hold it…I want you to see it. See how it beats.
Each new beat is a new opportunity. A new chance to be happy.
Breathe into your heart. See it fill up again. And let go. Let it
dissolve.

Open your eyes.

I suppose we should go back to work.
How do you feel about love?
What?
I know you heard the question.

What was your ex-girlfriend like?
I don't really want to talk about her.
Have you ever properly spoken about her since you broke up?

She was kind of perfect. Intelligent, kind, super funny. Cute. She
had the most adorable smile – it absolutely melted me. She'd
laugh at only my good jokes which I really appreciated. I
couldn't even try to muster a bad word to say about her if I
searched for one.
I still think about her everyday. Wonder what she's up to now.
I'll be doing something menial and I'll get lost, end up thinking
about her, wondering if she's doing the same thing.
Remembering how much better all the shit you have to do in life
was when she was there to do it with. The fog was cleared. It
always felt sunny. When it ended…It felt like I was never going
to be the same, like when she left so did part of me. God, I'm
lame aren't I?

What happened?

I happened.

I never thought I'd fall in love again. But then I met Clifford.
And everything changed. You're never out of hope.

We should get back to work.

Grief.
Lower back – a throbbing. It starts to cascade up your spine.
Torso is heavy. Desperate to topple over and sink into the
ground but you can't.
A lit candle at the top of a hill. The world around is perfectly
still. You start to approach and the world begins to shake –
the flame begins to flicker and –

I'm in the market for something new.
Hello there you tall drink of water.
As it stands I'm eternally disappointed with my current provider
and I want a change. I want to mix things up.
Let's see what we can do then.

Odd unit. One of those tall guys that never really came to terms
with the fact he's tall, slight slump in the shoulders, glasses –
well that's a little cliché – like Stephen Merchant with longer
features and kind of…Odder.

My partner lives in Hong Kong so I need lots of international call credit in whatever plan I go on.

…There are lots of free ways of calling overseas nowadays.

Yes. There are. If you spend your time with your eyes shut then those avenues might be the best ones for you.

Sorry?

Nothing in this life is free.

You're losing him.

Sure.

I don't think I follow.

That's exactly what they want?

Who?

The government.

Oh you've definitely lost him.

The government?

What do you think they do with all this international call data over your Whatsapp's and your Facetimes?

Nothing?

Fool. Darn fool.

What do they do?

Am I talking to an idiot?

Rough.

They harvest. Harvest information. And if they start harvesting information what's next? Organs? Oh no. I have a colleague he went on a business trip to Shanghai, fell asleep on the flight for an hour and woke up without his kidneys.

That's not true.

Are you calling me a liar?

Sounds like it.

In this instance I suppose I am.

How about you educate yourself you donkey faced dickhead?

How about you fuck off cunt?

I'm taking my business elsewhere.
Good.

See despite what you might think that's not actually the worst
end to an interaction one might expect. At it's core there was still
some level of civility.
Our friend here merely offered the retort of 'how about you fuck
off cunt?' in response to a very rude customer who'd insulted
him many times. What's also worth noting was that it was only a
suggestion. As Australian as it comes – doesn't even have the
linguistic confidence to follow through on a statement.

Yeah okay. Thanks.

Hey I'm trying to help.

You did just lose the un-losable sale there though.
Okay.
He came in asking to buy something.
Yes, but –
Sales is an interesting choice for you.
Another opportunity is always around –

Can I help you?
I'm just browsing.
Hunt.
For anything in particular?
No, not really.
You will not be defeated again.
The new Samsung…It's a cracker.
Yeah. Yeah so I've heard.

44

Well let me know if you need anything.

At least someone's *trying* to help customers.
What do Helga and Cliff do all day?
Administration.
All day?
I've got sales covered.
Prove it.
What?
Talk a big game.
Yeah?
Oh, look at that confidence. Interesting. What's that about?
It's cause I can deliver. You don't own me. I can do this.
Yet to really see it though aren't we?
Oh yeah?
Yeah.
Shit you really want this? I'll show it to you.
The floor's yours.
I'll wipe the fucking floor.

Recklessness.
Biceps. Surging, raging – the blood rushing up and down.
A drop top convertible on an open highway. Sun in your
eyes. Flying.

For reasons I can't explain sometimes I just feel like I could run
through a brick wall without a scratch.
I feel the blood coursing through my veins and it's pure lithium.
Nothing's getting in my way.

5G roaming capabilities with out of this world 8K video snap. Not only does it take stupidly good photos, it will change the way you take videos. Sleek, modern design which shits on all it's competitors – let me tell you guy…This phone is magic. This phone is a treasure. Do you need it? Maybe not. Do you want it? You sure as shit do. Cause we live in a world where what you want is what you can get and you can get this phone today. Right now. Leave this store with a new piece of your personality lighting up your pockets. You can be someone with this phone. We are what we eat my friend and the world is eating tech – if you don't start feasting then you'll fall behind and who will you be then? Weird uncle Errol the birdwatcher with a briefcase phone? No one wants that for you. Be here, be now, be somebody.

Okay.
Okay?
Sounds good.

Cool. If you see one of my colleagues they'll sort out your details.
Okay.

You. Are. Amazing.
I'm impressed.
Yeah cause I'm fucking impressive.
He was stunned.
Credit where credit's due, man.
Did you see his face? I could've convinced that dude to blow a horse and he would have said neigh.
Wait, what?

Neigh as in horse neigh not nay as in nay –
Butchered the dismount there.
Whatever, you're not robbing me of this. I'm hot shit right now.
This is good stuff man.
I'm Jesus.
Dude. Jesus is dead.
Yeah and I'm not!
Are you saying you're better than Jesus?
Did Jesus ever sell a Samsung Galaxy?
NOPE!
I reckon Jesus had you covered in sales just quietly. You still
have to pay tax.
Where's the next one?
People! Where you at? This dude's flying.
Soaring.

And just like that…Fucken stop me.
The best part of hypomania is that you feel like you could do
anything.
The worst part is that you know there's another side to it.

Helga, I just had this insane spiel about how he would basically
become a better person with this phone and although that is
probably antithetical to my like life philosophy I still feel really
great – also that's interesting right – I'm in sales but there's this
push and pull – I want to believe that this is a job and that if I
didn't do it then someone else would but at the same time I'm
just continuing this neo-liberal economic, you know, and that's
whatever – what does neo-liberal mean again – I may be mixing
up my – doesn't matter – do you know what I mean?

Not…Entirely.

Ha. Neither. So, like, yeah…Yeah…Interesting.
What?
Huh?
What's interesting?
Oh. Life. When something seems like something but really it's
something else.
Am I supposed to understand what you're saying…?
That could be hard, Helga, as I don't understand what I'm saying
necessarily. Holy shit it feels good to be here!

Here?
I don't want to take things for granted anymore. Positive strides.

If you knew what it was like to feel this…
You wouldn't take the meds.

What are the chances?
Lucy. Hi.
You work at Vodafone now?
Um.

I…
Solar plexus.
You're anxious.
Are you looking for um…How are you?
I'm really good thanks. And you?

Were you after a plan?
Yeah.
Solar plexus.
You still get –
Yeah.
Starts in your –
Yeah.
Why didn't you fight harder?
What else is – what what what's news?
I got made partner at my firm.
Dickhead of the year letting her go.
That's so – I thought you were too young to – but you really
deserve that – I'm happy for you. Not that you need me – or even
want me to be happy for you – but I am. Do you need a new
phone or just the plan?
Just the plan I got the phone outright.
New iPhone. Nice. Is that an engraving? B and L.
Yeah…Ben and Lucy…

You're going out with – you and Ben are –
Little under a year.
Fucking wow! Amazing!
You don't have to be okay with it.
Why wouldn't I be? Ben's such an amazing…

What started in the solar plexus creeps up your chest – spreads
across your shoulders – constricts your throat –

We're engaged actually. Obviously this isn't how I wanted you
to find out.

Are you –
The ring! Yeah!
Anyway enough about me are you seeing anyone?
Oh yeah.
Great. Who is she?
She's um…She's a real estate agent. She grew up in Canberra
but moved to Sydney after Uni. She's twenty nine.
Kind of just sounds like you're reading out her Bumble profile.

Laughs.

Yeah…I'm not. Like, we hang out sometimes – well twice,
we've hung out – we've been on two dates – two promising
dates. Going on one tonight actually so…Who knows? Love, um,
it could be around the corner – in your shop. About to be – I'm
going to hand you over to Cliff over there who can take you
through the…Ins and outs…Of the…Whole thing…

I just need a second.
Sure. Nice to see you.

You should kill yourself.
I can't do this right now – she's there.
Not now. After work.
Senses.
Do it. You've imagined it so many –
Senses.
So many times –
What can you see?
Um.
It must be exhausting.
The fluorescent light bouncing off the plastic phone covers.
What can you hear?

And how boring to fight everyday.
Helga clicking her pen.
Smell.

I can't smell anything.

Can you name what you're feeling?

No.

Just give up and this'll all be over.

Hey nice to see you. Thanks for looking after me.
Oh yeah, you got the – you're all sorted?
Yep.

Your colleagues seem to really care about you.
Uh-huh.

They're um…

Nice people.

Okay…Well…Bye.
Bye.

Look after yourself.

Senses.

Her eyes.
This is a bad idea.
Senses.
Her laugh.
Don't say I didn't warn you.
Senses.
The smell of sea salt in her hair – that um – that spray she used –
You're on your own here.
Not memories – senses.

Agony.
Fingers and toes. They begin to curl in, unable to take the crushing... The weight.
You as a small child. You're smiling. But you know you're not happy. You reach to comfort yourself –

How long do you want the war to rage on?

How many more hours do you want to put into surviving the onslaught?

The only shame in caving is the time it's already taken.

When you're born you have no concept of who you're going to be. You have genetic foundations and then programming kicks in when you become cognizant. Your surrounds make up who you are.

It's okay to admit defeat in the eyes of…You wouldn't even call this defeat it's…Home.

You're just…Un-loveable.

Excuse me, Helga, Cliff – I'm ah, I'm feeling a little under the weather.
Tummy trouble? We have some Diarrhea relief tablets in the first aid kit.
No it's a bit beyond that.
We've all done it. Go clean yourself up.
No, I haven't shat myself…I need to get out of here.

Okay then. See you tomorrow.
See you tomorrow.

Eighty nine steps to freedom.
Fluorescent lights beaming down on you. They feel like they're burning holes in your skin – shards of piercing light cracking you open.
Drops of Jupiter is careering around the shopping centre and you realize that the joy you got from this song, albeit ironically, has totally disappeared and Train are really just Nickleback meets Keith Urban for Nova listeners and you hate yourself for being that kind of wanker that can't enjoy simple pleasures like a catchy mediocre song – THEY'RE NOT GOING TO PLAY RADIOHEAD IN A SHOPPING CENTRE!

Black.
The sun. You look at it for too long.
It's not black.

No that's black.
Spots.
You shouldn't stare at the sun. You're not a flower.
If I do enough acid I could be.
Getting sick of me yet? You know how to get rid of me.
It's okay to distract yourself.

Lucy is engaged on Facebook – I must've missed that.
Not Facebook.
What is wrong with you?
Ben just got a promotion too.
I thought I told you to get off Facebook.
This is Instagram now.
Good for him.
Fuckwit.
Could've been you.
They look so happy together. I was a dead weight.
Get off socials!

Solar plexus.

Christ.

I'll rattle off some options.
Hanging – proven method. Could be long.
Jumping – Kinda scary.
Train – Splat. Takes open casket out of the question.

Wow this is a real smorgasbord of suicide.
An entrée of expiration.
A delicatessen of death.
Does it come with a pickle on the side?
If it doesn't then I'm never coming back.

I hate to break it to you –
It's only a matter of time.
Let go.

Is it wrong that the feeling of weeping feels so satisfying?
This is feeling.
Evidence I'm alive.
I can feel the weight of my tears running down my face.
Taste the salt.
Hear my breath rattle in my chest – my body desperately
searching for more oxygen.

Someone's going to be a fun date.
You should cancel.
Fuck.
'Hi, nice to see you again – do you mind if I cry through dinner?'
Don't subject someone else to this…

Phone a friend!
This isn't 'Who wants to be a millionaire' – he's a wet sock.
What does a conversation with him entail? I – I – I – I feel sad.
Cry, cry, cry.

If you had a car you could gas yourself.

As you step onto the bus you think…Am I the crazy person who
cries on the bus?
The answer is categorical – yes.
You try and avoid eye contact – not that anyone wants to look at
you.
It's a sad indictment on society when –
Who am I kidding? As if I'd talk to a crying dude on a bus. Even
though a couple of kind words could –

Is my stop ever going to come?
Get me off this bus.
Please don't sit in front of me.

Excuse me…Are you okay?

Thank you.

I'm fine.

She can probably feel my hot sobbing breath punching into the
back of her neck.
Stop breathing.

I'm going to throw up.
Not on the fucking bus.

Burps.

Sorry.

Charming.
This is your stop.
What?
Your stop! Your stop!
Oh shit.
Press the button.
I was –
Press it!
I have pressed it!

He was trying not to throw up.
I was trying not to throw up.

That was your stop.
I know that was my stop. You made it perfectly clear that was
my stop.
It's only another hundred metres.
The exercise wouldn't hurt.

Fresh air.
Sort of fresh.
The fumes of the cars pissing at you make the term 'fresh' a little
loose.
The chaos stops the tears.

Feet hitting the pavement. Heel and toe. Pressing into the
ground. Pain down the outside of your left knee. A little
discomfort in your lower back, right side. Shoulders are tight.
Slight throbbing in the front of your head.

You should try heroin. I've heard good things.
Hendrix. Joplin. Cobaine.
Must be something to it if they all loved it that much.
They all died from it.
Cobaine was a shotgun.
High on heroin.
Might be worth a think is all I'm saying.
Then you wouldn't have to care anymore.
You could just take up stealing stuff and dribbling.
Dribbling on the side of the road without a care in the world.

Bus screeching out from the curb. Cars passing, one hits the
breaks with a little too much vigor. A bird, calling out – no
response. Your breath, loud enough to hear it. Trees rustling.

Kill yourself.

White lines on the road, broken up. Cars. Um. Cars. Shit. You're
no good at this.

Kill yourself.

White lines on the road. Cars.

Kill yourself.

Cars.
Cars.
Cars.
Cars.
Jump.
Cars.

Home.

I like how you're doing your exercises – it's cute.
Shower.

A reward for a big day of –
Sweet fuck all.
A coping –
Hardly call it coping –
A tool to build –
Crumbling little man.

Hotter.
It's burning.

Hotter.
I can't.
Hotter.

Steam – filling the shower – steam – shit.
You dry yourself off and get into running gear. It seems
counterintuitive but you're at a loss at this point. Nothing's
making sense.

You go outside and…

I'm running. I don't know where I'm going or how long I'm
going to last. Every step feels like…I'm running in humus. I
don't even like – whatever – the analogy is what it is, you get the
drift.
I'm so exhausted but there's this reserve of energy – I'm willing
it to die. To dry up. But it's taking you everywhere, it's all that's
keeping you going.
Before I know it I'm on this busy street, I know the street, the
name – I've been here a thousand times but the name…there are
people everywhere.
People are laughing and holding hands and a couple at the traffic
lights are kissing and I'm overcome with…rage.
I picture myself hitting him in the face – clobbering him – for no
other reason than…he's happy.
But I'm gone now – I've kept running. Maybe this distraction is
working.
I can barely breathe, my mouth is so dry it feels like each breath
is passing through sandpaper to get to my lungs.
I'm in a park. Alone. The sun's going down.
I lie down in the grass – it itches but I don't mind. I can hardly
focus on anything other than…

The tears and the sweat dripping down my back – if it was beautiful I'd say it was cascading but it isn't – there's nothing beautiful – it's collecting in my butt crack, tickling my asshole. Lovely.
And for a moment I can see it – joy. I'm crying so hard and all I want to do is itch my asshole but I'm so fucking exhausted I can't be bothered – I'm so tired, so - I rub my arse on the ground like a randy little mutt. And this is what I've become.

It's funny. All this – I know it's funny.
But the thought of laughing feels entirely alien.
The promise of light is always overshadowed by the power of darkness.

I'd do anything not to give it power.

All these tricks, distractions, tools – all an attempt to stop this hideous inertia. Unstoppable cunting force of…

The sun's gone.
My chest has been heaving so much from the sobbing that I've made an impression in the grass – like it's holding me. Or doing it's best to push me away.
I sit up and remember I'm alone.

And late.
Shit.
I'm late. Why didn't you tell me?
We wanted to let you have your moment.
She'll be waiting –
Hurry up then.

Adrenaline.
Less time to think.
No time for a shower.

Hang on –
Do you want to be late or a little smelly?

Late.

Shower number three.
You know we're in a drought?
I thought that was over.
Safe to assume we'll always be in drought.
The psychologist said –
It's an exercise. We know. It's just, you know, the betterment of
society you're neglecting.

Shower.
Clothes.
Deep breaths.
Concentration.
Confidence.
Cowardice.
Cologne.
The sweet smell of Hugo Boss.
Another antisemite.
It was a gift.
Mummy's favourite scent.

Get moving.

You're about to enter the restaurant where you're meeting a
woman who you've come to fancy quite a lot when you realize –
Asian fusion – spicy food – you're wearing a grey shirt.
You're sweating in anticipation.
It'll be fine. Separate orders. Just order something mild.
God she looks good and you look -

Sorry I'm late.

Did you run here?

The armpits? No that's just one of my quirks. You should see my undies! You don't want to see my undies. Not because there's anything down there. I mean there is something down there but nothing, like, everything that should be there is there and anything that shouldn't isn't so – no surprises. It's funny I'm wearing Alpha undies actually, I bought them at K-Mart, um, I'm telling you that because...I knew it was funny for some reason – oh yeah cause I'm like not alpha at all so...

Have you had a look at the menu?

Yeah. Do you think we should just get a couple of mains to share?

....Yep.

Great. I'm thinking we get the spicy tofu salad, the jungle curry and the spicy pork belly – is that okay with you?

Wonderful. Great order.

You've been well?

Yes. I have. Really well.

That's good.

I've had a couple of bumps actually but I think I've handled them quite well. Adjusting.

Her eyes.

Disarming. Terrifyingly so.

Any protective coating is melting away.

Like my heart is wrapped in wax and her eyes the scorching heat. I know I should be saying something rather than just staring but I'm bereft of words, barely able to stop myself from the dizziness – what's happening to me?

You look around the room but those eyes –
They lock you in.
And you're –
Caught up –
In her.

You have to say something.

I think you're wonderful.
That's very nice of you.
Sorry that just – it slipped out – how have you been?
Yeah…Good…Honestly it's actually been a pretty hard week. I found out my dad's got cancer so –
Oh fuck. That's, I mean, that's not what you want.
…No.
What a shit, shit, how are you – do you like him?
My dad?
I phrased that badly. I'm a bit – do you get on well?
Not particularly but he's my Dad so it's still a bit –
Right –
Obviously it's still a bit –
It's a bit shit –
No, no, it's worse than that.
Totally. It's totally shit. I mean it's cancer and judging by how you said it's probably terminal which is…Even shitter.

It sure is.

I don't normally drink on weeknights but I might order a cocktail – would you like a drink?
I can't actually. I guess I should tell you – I'm an alcoholic.
Really? Never would've, wow, there you go.

63

Seven months sober.
Congratulations.

Alcoholic with a dying dad – she's still coming up trumps.

What was your rock bottom?
Oh…
You hear that don't you? That there's a moment, a rock bottom, a moment so disgraceful or embarrassing that you don't have a choice but to change.
Yeah…
Probably not what you want to be talking about I guess.
Not really. But since you asked –
You don't have to –
No. I should own my past.

There'd been…Many things that had let up to the point where enough was enough. I had my best friend's birthday one night and my ex was invited. Um. I can get socially, a little anxious. I drank all day in preparation. I was totally black out by the time I got there. And within half an hour of being there…I'd thrown up all over myself. I passed out and landed on the concrete, split my head open. Got twenty three stitches in my skull. And my friend, it was the last straw for her. I'm trying to rekindle that friendship but…

And the sensible part of me knew I should've stopped there but I didn't. I felt so disgusted and ashamed of myself that I went on a bender for…A few weeks. Probably. I don't know the exact time frame. It all got a little…I got sacked. And I remember sitting in my apartment, with no job, no friends and a bottle of tequila in front of me and thinking…If I keep going like this…I'll die.

Good on you.

For seeking help. Lesser people wouldn't.

Are you ready to order?
Yes.

Dinner's flying past and you can barely catch it. You're wrapped
up in every word, wondering if tonight you'll get a kiss,
wondering what life looks like with her. How all the boring stuff
would be so much less boring. Going to the supermarket, doing
laundry, anything, anything, but as long as she's there. Will we
kiss?
Where did it all go?
All that time.

That was...I really like you.

So...

Never a good sign.

You're a lovely guy.
Complicated is more accurate.
And I can see you've got a good heart.
You don't need to –
No, I want to.
What the fuck? She wants to what? Crush your soul even more.

I think you'll make someone really happy, I honestly do.
Too much emphasis.
I just don't think we're compatible.

Sorry was that the end?
Yeah that was about it.
Oh, okay. Well…Thanks for letting me know. A prompt
response time to whether or not you could fall in love with me is
always appreciated.

Joke.
Yes.

Can I ask you something?
Sure.
Was it anything in particular that I did?

My last boyfriend had some pretty bad mental health problems. I
know how this sounds but…I just don't have the energy.
It's…Work.
I never told you I had mental health problems.

Thank you for a lovely dinner.

You watch her leave and you can't help but wonder…Was that
the last chance to find the love of my life?

You really fucked that up. At some point you have to ask
yourself…
What is wrong with me? Why can't I just be normal?
We land on this a bit don't we?

I really did like her.
So did I.
It's hard to continue to muster the energy.
Can't feel good.
Twitching.
How's the heart?
Twitching.
Crushing

It could be so easy.

Traffic.
Train.
Booze.
Hanging.
Jumping.
Gassing.
Slitting.
Stabbing.
Shooting.

Maybe there's…What's the point dancing around all this?
You're just using up oxygen you don't deserve. Another day
filled with constant, unrelenting hopelessness. And you, you just
don't shut the fuck up, do you?
Nope.
Have it your way then.
WHY CAN'T I BE NORMAL?

Kill yourself.
At least I wouldn't have to listen to -

No.
No.
NO.
NO.
NO.
NO!
NO!

Please. Please. Please. Please. Please. Please. Please. Please.
Please. Please. Please. Please. Please.
PLEASE. PLEASE. PLEASE. PLEASE. PLEASE. PLEASE.
PLEASE. PLEASE. PLEASE. PLEASE. PLEASE. PLEASE.

Rage.
Floating rib. Stabbing. No. Shanking.
Tickle in the nostril. Insatiable.
Eyebrow lifting. Yanking.

Blue flame piercing pig flesh. Ripping through the body so fast it disintegrates.

Kill yourself.

You make it home even though you thought you wouldn't.

And once again…You start to weep.

I don't know how much longer I can do this.
It must be exhausting.

I'm exhausted and I'm just in your head.

The weight of your misery wrenches your shoulders.
Let them drop.
Go with it.
You're on the floor.
Sobbing.

It must be exhausting.

Minutes, hours, days, weeks, years, all adding up. You're
overwhelmed by it now. The inertia. The relentless pain. The
search for joy has dried up. All you feel is hatred. How could
anyone ever love you when you hate yourself so much?

You're home now.
It's okay.
If there's ever a time to do it…
It's okay.

And suddenly, as if you're punched in the face by it – clarity.

So much of your life has been spent wishing. Wishing that things
were different. Wishing that you were different. Time spent with
friends, they're faces lit up with smiles and laughter and you,
behind a pane of glass wondering how they do it. You want to
join them but you're being pushed away. And you wish and wish
and wish but you're…Wishes can come true.

I'm exhausted.

Calmly, you stand. Make your way to the bathroom. The mirror.
Quetiapine. Sleeping pills. Recently filled prescription.
Lorazepam. Slow release anxiety meds. Over half the bottle left.
Thanks for the fifty bottle.
Diazepam. Nine left.
That should do it.

You walk to the kitchen. It feels strange how calm you feel.
Resolute.

What's the poison?
Vodka?
Gin?
Tequila. That's the upper alcohol.

Maybe the coroner will see the humour in it.

You glide towards the living room carrying three pill bottles and
a bottle of cheap tequila.
You sit on the couch. Make yourself comfortable.

You open all three pill bottles and pour them on the coffee table
in front of you like they're from a packet of mixed M & M's.
You take a gulp from the tequila bottle.

The agonizing pain of cheap tequila doesn't even register.
You swig again, deeper now.

You grab a handful of the pills –
A mixed bag.

You put your hand to your mouth when –

His phone rings.

Hi Mum.
Yeah…I was going to call you back I just…
It didn't go well, Mum.

I know there are but I really liked her.

It just hurts, I guess.

No, no, I'm fine. I'm okay. I'm fine.

It's good to hear your voice.

No plans for the rest of the night. Maybe a bit of Netflix. I
couldn't get into it. Yeah I love Eugene Levy too. Just not my
poison this one.

I'm gonna jump in the shower, Mum. I've had a big day.

I love you too.

Relief.
Whole body. A warm breeze gently rolling across your skin.
The ocean. Waves trickling in. In and out. The sound of the
water caressing the sand. The foam of the waves latching
onto every granule before slowly melting away.

The sobbing stops.

The pills can go away now.
Won't need them tonight.
Got close that time.
But you didn't.

Temporary pause in proceedings.
But a pause nonetheless.
We'll always be here.
A roar may turn into a whisper.

Your head hits the pillow.
You're exhausted.
You close your eyes and finally –
You fall into a deep sleep.

Finally.

Peace.

You made it.

Rest. Recharge your resilience. You made it.

Tomorrow. A new chance for hope. A new chance for change.
I'll live to fight another day.

THE END

<u>Other plays by Xavier Coy:</u>

The Great Emu War

Smokin' Joe

Caught Out

Are You Listening Now?

Distorted

Charles & Larry

<u>Coming soon:</u>

Not Even God Can Save Us

Together

The Coleslaw Conundrum

The King's Cross

Teamwork

First Christmas

Agency

The World According To Jerry

ORiGiN™
Theatrical

FOR ALL ENQUIRIES CONTACT: ORiGiN™ Theatrical
PO BOX Q1235, QVB Post Office, Sydney, NSW, 1230, Australia
Phone: (61 2) 8514 5201
enquiries@originmusic.com.au
www.origintheatrical.com.au
Part of the ORiGiN™ Music Group
An Australian Independent Music Company

www.ingramcontent.com/pod-product-compliance
Lightning Source LLC
Chambersburg PA
CBHW060056100426
42742CB00014B/2850